Family World

My Dad

Caryn Jenner

W
FRANKLIN WATTS
LONDON • SYDNEY

Sharing this book

This book shows the variety of roles that a father plays in children's lives around the world. It provides a useful starting point to discuss how families everywhere are similar, but that each child's family is different and special.

• Remember that families are formed in different ways and a father can be a step-father, an adoptive father, a foster father or anyone else that the child thinks of as a father.
• Being a dad is a rewarding job, but sometimes it can be difficult. Ask your GP, health visitor or school for advice.

These organisations also offer help to families:
Family Lives – www.familylives.org.uk Parentline 0808 800 2222
Family Links – www.familylinks.org.uk
Gingerbread (especially for single-parent families) – www.gingerbread.org.uk

First published in 2013 by Franklin Watts
Copyright © Franklin Watts 2013

Franklin Watts
338 Euston Road
London NW1 3BH

Franklin Watts Australia
Level 17/207 Kent Street
Sydney, NSW 2000

Series Editor: Sarah Peutrill
Series Designer: Ruth Walton

Dewey number: 306.8'742
ISBN: 978 1 4451 1929 8
Printed in Malaysia

Franklin Watts is a division of Hachette Children's Books, an Hachette UK company. www.hachette.co.uk

Please note: Some of the pictures in this book are posed by models. All scenarios are fictitious and any similarities to people, living or dead, are purely coincidental.

Picture credits: AISPIX by Image Source/Shutterstock: back cover. 10c. Yuri Arcurs/Shutterstock: 23c. Atlas pix/Shutterstock: 19t. Judy Barracnco/istockphoto: 16tr. beboy/Shutterstock: 23cr. Peter Bernik/Shutterstock: 12cl. Christophe Boisson/Shutterstock: 8tl. Michel Borges/Shutterstock: 23bc. c/Shutterstock: 4t, 19c. Augusto Cabral/Shutterstock: 6cb, 15clt, 16tc. J Carillet/istockphoto: 5tr. Sophie Louise Davis/Shutterstock: 23tlc. Sanjay Deva/Shutterstock: 23bl. Martine Doucet/istockphoto: 14c. Brian Eichhorn//Shutterstock: 23tl. Elena Elisseeva/Shutterstock: 23clc, Fotogroove/Shutterstock: 14t. gabor2100/Shutterstock: 20-21. Tatiana Gladskikh/istockphoto: 16bl. Glenda/Shutterstock: 19b. Globe Turner/Shutterstock: 5cl, 9tc, 10cr. adam golabek/Shutterstock: 9cl. llike/Shutterstock: 11c. Kamira/Shutterstock: 12b. Shane Kato/istockphoto: 7tr. Aleksey Klints/Shutterstock: 11t. Kzenon/Shutterstock: 19tb. Geir Olav Lyngfjell/Shutterstock: 22. margusson/Shutterstock: 18t. megastocker/Shutterstock: 15trb. mojito.mak[dog]gmail[dot]com/Shutterstock: 17c. Monkey Business/Shutterstock: 5b, 15tr. Odua Images/Shutterstock: 9tr. OLJ Studio/Shutterstock: 23cl. PT Images/Shutterstock: 23tc, 23tr. rehoboth photo/Shutterstock: 10cl, 13t. SeanShot/istockphoto: 4c. Jane September/Shutterstock,: 9bl. Mark Spowart/istockphoto: 15cl. Topanga/Shutterstock: 7bl. tuulijumala/Shutterstock: 16blb. Dana Ward/Shutterstock: 18b. wavebreakmedia/Shutterstock: 12c. Piotr Wawrzyniuk/Dreamstime: 7cl. Jim West/Alamy: 13c. Micky Wiswedel/istockphoto: 6c. Catherine Yeulet/istockphoto: front cover, 17t. Lisa F. Young/Shutterstock: 10bl. Zurijeta/Shutterstock: 8c.Every attempt has been made to clear copyright. Should there be any inadvertent omission please apply to the publisher for rectification.

Contents

This is my dad

Think about your dad and the things you do together. All over the world, fathers love their children and look after them.

Sam lives in Britain. This is his dad. He helps Sam choose books at the library.

Desta is from Ethiopia. She calls her dad 'Abaye'. Desta likes holding his hand.

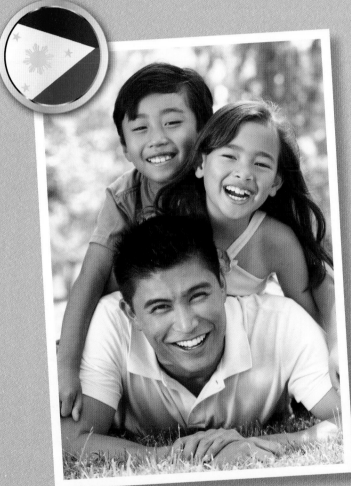

In the Philippines, Tala and Rafael call their dad "Tatay". They love to climb on him!

? **What do you call your dad?**

Caring for me

Fathers look after their children in lots of different ways. They make sure their children sleep, eat and stay healthy.

Jeso's dad reads him a bedtime story in South Africa. He makes sure Jeso gets plenty of sleep.

In Denmark, Lisbet's parents adopted her and they became a family. Today, Lisbet and her dad shop for healthy food to eat.

Petra's family lives in Slovakia. Her dad looks after her when she is ill. Soon Petra will be healthy again.

How does your dad care for you?

Having fun together

Fathers can be fun to play with.

Murat lives with his family in Turkey. He likes colouring pictures with his dad. His brother and sister like it too.

In Australia, Daniel's step-dad is married to his mother. On holiday Daniel and his step-dad floated down a river in a big raft!

In China, Song Yi's dad takes her swimming once a week.

How do you and your dad have fun together?

Acting Silly

Fathers are often brilliant at acting silly and making children laugh.

In Indonesia, Hani and her brother, Adit, tickle their dad and they all laugh like crazy!

Dan lives in the United States with his two dads. They all get silly when they watch American football on TV.

Oleg is from Russia. He likes to arm-wrestle with his dad. Sometimes, Oleg wins!

What kinds of silly things do you do with your dad?

Teaching me

Children have a lot to learn, and fathers can help.

In the Netherlands, Ruben's dad teaches him to ride his bicycle.

Luisa and her dad live in Brazil. He helps Luisa with homework. He's especially good at maths.

Dana is learning to play baseball in the United States. Her dad shows her how to swing the bat.

What does your dad teach you?

Working together

There's always work to do, and sometimes children can help their fathers.

In Italy, Rosana and her brother, Tito, visit their dad at weekends. At his house, they all cook dinner together.

Brody and his dad do the washing at their home in New Zealand. Brody likes the smell of fresh washing.

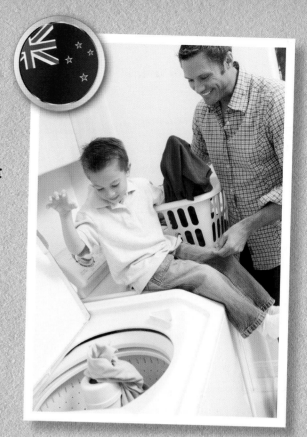

Troy lives on a farm in Canada. He often works in the fields with his dad.

Sometimes you need to keep yourself busy while your dad gets on with the work.

Comforting me

When children feel sad, fathers try to comfort them to make them feel better.

Courtney is starting a new school in Canada. She feels a bit nervous until her dad makes her smile.

Diego's family is from Puerto Rico. When Diego feels sad, his dad helps by listening and comforting him.

In Belgium, Michelle feels cosy and safe when her dad gives her a cuddle.

Think of a time when your dad comforted you. What did he do to make you feel better?

Being together

Just spending time together is a good way for fathers and children to show that they love each other.

Faisal's family lives in Afghanistan. Faisal likes being with his dad. Sometimes they talk, and sometimes it's just good to be together.

Marianne and Giselle are from France. They like kicking a football around with their dad.

In Britain, Rohit's dad makes him – and his new baby sister – feel special.

How do you feel when you and your dad are together?

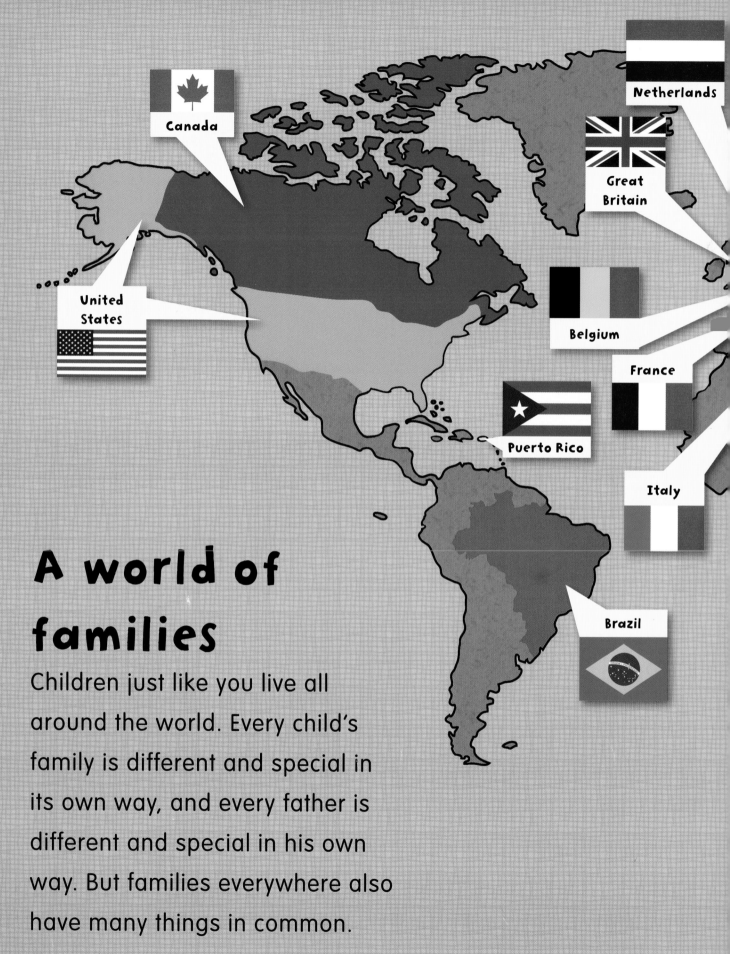

A world of families

Children just like you live all around the world. Every child's family is different and special in its own way, and every father is different and special in his own way. But families everywhere also have many things in common.

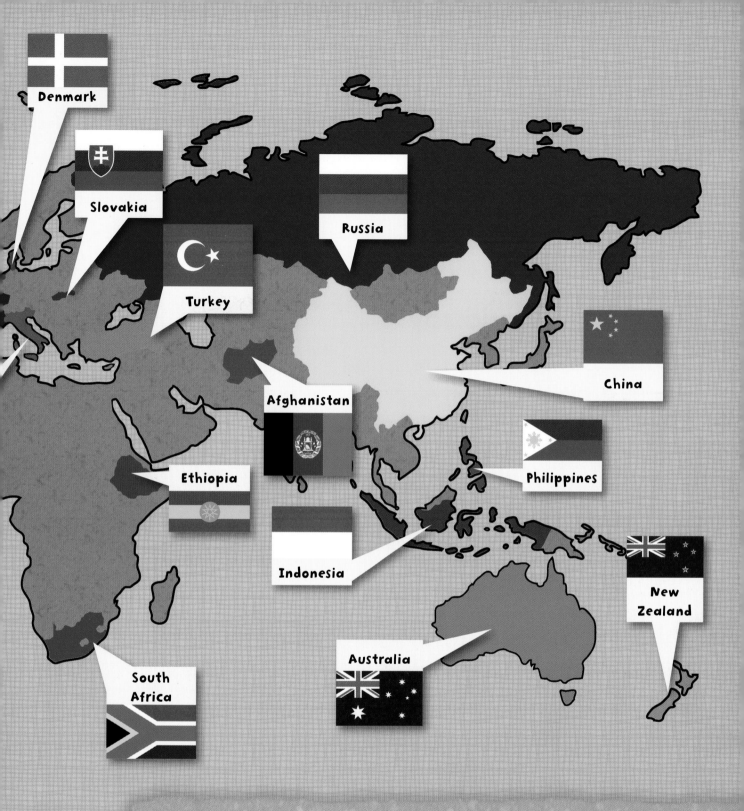

The families in this book live in the countries marked on this map. Can you find the flag that goes with each family in the book?

Activities

Tell your dad why he's special

Make an award certificate for him. Write 'I think you're special because…' or 'You're brilliant because…' and list the things he does that you think are special.

Find out how children around the world say 'father'.

Find out how to say father in different languages. Ask friends who speak other languages, or look it up in books or on the Internet. Here are a few languages to get you started:

Spanish – Padre   French – Père
Urdu – Abbu   Polish – Tata
Chinese – Baba   Japanese – Otosan

Pretend to be a dad

Play a dressing-up game. Pretend you are a dad while your dad pretends he is a child. Pretend to do the things that he usually does for you, such as comforting him if he gets hurt or tucking him in bed. You can get ideas from this book.

Make a family tree

A family tree shows the people in your family. Draw a picture of yourself and each person in your family, or use photos. On another sheet of paper, draw a tree. Stick your family pictures onto your tree. Your family tree can show the people you live with, or it can show lots of people in your family. You can even include your pets!

Granny and Grandad
(Mum's parents)

Grandma and Grandpa
(Dad's parents)

Mum

My aunt
(Mum's little sister)

My aunt
(Dad's big sister)

Dad

Me!

My sister

Words about families

Here are some words you may use when talking about families.

Adopted – becoming part of a family that is not the family you were born into

Divorced – when parents split up and are no longer married

Family – a group of people who love and care for each other and are usually related

Foster mum or dad – grown-ups who look after you in their family if your parents can't

Grandparents – your mum and dad's parents

Half-brother or half-sister – a brother or sister who has the same mum or dad as you, but the other parent is different

Parents – your mum and dad

Siblings – brothers and sisters

Step-brother or step-sister – the son or daughter of your step-mum or step-dad

Step-mum or step-dad – if your parents are divorced and one of them marries again, the new wife or husband would be your step-mum or step-dad

Index